PRESIDENTIAL WIT & WISDOM

13-Digit ISBN: 978-1-60433-609-2
10-Digit ISBN: 1-60433-609-9

Appleseed Press Book Publishers
68 North Street
Kennebunkport, Maine 04046

Visit us online at
appleseedpressbooks.com

Typography: Minion, Nexa Rust Slab

Photo credits:
Presidential collage: Andrew Jackson (Shutterstock), Theodore Roosevelt (Library of Congress), Zachary Taylor (Shutterstock), George W. Bush (Wikimedia Commons), George Washington (Library of Congress), John F. Kennedy (NARA), Thomas Jefferson (Shutterstock), Ronald Reagan (NARA), and Barack Obama (Library of Congress).

Library of Congress: pages 10, 14, 16, 22, 23, 29, 30, 34, 37, 39, 40, 45, 47, 48, 53, 54, 55, 56, 58, 59, 60, 63, 65, 66, 69, 70, 74, 75, 78, 80, 83, 84, 86, 91 (photo by Marion S. Trikosko), 94, 97, 98, 100, 103, 109, 117, 118, 121, 122, 125, 126, 129, 135, 136, 139, 146, 151, 155, 157, 162, 166, 171, 177, 179, 180, 181, 183, 184, 185, 186, 187, 188, 189, 190, 191.

Shutterstock (Everett Historical): pages 13, 17, 19, 25, 26, 32, 51, 72, 76, 79, 89, 95, 106, 110, 113, 114, 128, 130, 140, 143, 144, 148, 152, 156, 169, 170, 173, 174.

Shutterstock: pages 20, 132, 159, 160.

Shutterstock (Susan Law Cain): page 42.

Wikimedia Commons: pages 49 and 165.

National Archives and Records Administration: pages 50, 88, and 93.

Shutterstock (Stocksnapper): page 102.

Shutterstock (Victorian Traditions): page 104.

Printed in China

1 2 3 4 5 6 7 8 9 0
First Edition

PRESIDENTIAL
WIT & WISDOM

More Than 200 Classic Quotes
from America's Greatest Leaders

EDITED BY CHARLOTTE LEE GROSS

APPLESEED
· PRESS ·

· BOOK ·
PUBLISHERS

KENNEBUNKPORT, MAINE

"Be sincere;
be brief;
be seated."

FRANKLIN D. ROOSEVELT

CONTENTS

★INTRODUCTION★

INTRODUCTION

The president of the United States has, perhaps, the ultimate soapbox. The ears of millions of Americans, not to mention the attention of the world, are tuned to what such a leader has to say. For those of us listening to their official speeches and casual remarks, there are occasions to seize on presidential gaffes and misspoken words. But we can also catch glimpses of true insight. Sometimes, as in the case of Thomas Jefferson, a president might not speak well but writes with great eloquence. Whatever the case may be, there is no doubt that the legacy of the office is one rich in words and stories.

Whether you are a staunch Republican, firmly a Democrat, or something in between, there is much to be gained from reading the words of our past presidents. The differences in their opinions and approaches are enriched when allowed to speak to each other across the pages.

Similar respect for uniting values of courage, leadership, democracy, family, and humor transcend political boundaries. After all, didn't Reagan enjoy a good quip as much as Kennedy? Didn't Democrat Buchanan see the Constitution as absolutely foundational, just like Republican Ford did? Polk put it well when he said that the president must be chosen from a political party, "yet in his official action he should not be the President of a party only, but of the whole people of the United States." In much the same way, though the president sometimes speaks as a member of a party, he—or she!—speaks to all the people of the United States. In this spirit, I invite you to learn from, think about, and laugh with—or at—the words of our nation's executive leaders.

★ ★ ★ ★ ★ ★ ★ ★

Abraham Lincoln as *The Rail Splitter* by J. L. G. Ferris, ca. 1909.

★ CHARACTER ★

On personal qualities and how
(or how not) to act

★ COURAGE ★

"The only thing we have to fear is fear itself."

FRANKLIN D. ROOSEVELT, FIRST INAUGURAL ADDRESS, 1931

"By acting as if I was not afraid,
I gradually ceased to be afraid."

THEODORE ROOSEVELT

"Adhere to your purpose and you will soon
feel as well as you ever did.
On the contrary, if you falter, and give up,
you will lose the power of keeping any resolution,
and will regret it all your life."

ABRAHAM LINCOLN, LETTER TO QUINTIN CAMPBELL, JUNE 28, 1862

Theodore Roosevelt and General Leonard Wood.

Millard Fillmore refused to accept the honorary degree Oxford offered hi
"I have not the advantage of a classical education, and no man should,
in my judgment, accept a degree he cannot read," he said.
He added that Oxford students might not appreciate the awarding
of such an honor, saying, "They would probably ask, 'Who's Fillmore?
What's he done? Where did he come from?' And then my name would,
I fear, give them an excellent opportunity to make jokes at my expense.'

"I leave it to you. If I had another face,
do you think I would wear this one?"

ABRAHAM LINCOLN, TURNING TO THE AUDIENCE WHEN
STEPHEN A. DOUGLAS CALLED HIM "TWO-FACED" IN A DEBATE

"Perhaps one of the most important accomplishments
of my administration has been minding my own business."

CALVIN COOLIDGE IN HIS LAST PRESS CONFERENCE
BEFORE LEAVING OFFICE, MARCH 1, 1929

"It was absolutely involuntary.
They sank my boat."

JOHN F. KENNEDY, WHEN ASKED HOW HE BECAME A WAR HERO

"Here lie the bones of my old horse, 'General,'
Who served his master faithfully for twenty-one years,
And never made a blunder.
Would that his master could say the same!"

JOHN TYLER, EPITAPH ON THE GRAVESTONE OF HIS HORSE

★ ★ ★ ★ ★ ★ ★ ★ ★ ★

"We must adjust to changing times
and still hold to unchanging principles."

JIMMY CARTER

"Knowing what's right doesn't mean much
unless you do what's right."

THEODORE ROOSEVELT

"Always vote for principle, though you may vote alone,
and you may cherish the sweetest reflection
that your vote is never lost."

JOHN QUINCY ADAMS

"Labor to keep alive in your breast
that little spark of celestial fire
called conscience."

GEORGE WASHINGTON

★ ★ ★ ★ ★ ★ ★ ★

LITTLE DID YOU KNOW . . .

Not only was George Washington
the only president to lead troops into battle
while serving as president, he was also awarded
the highest rank in the U. S. military.
He received the honor posthumously,
but as General of the Armies of the United States,
no one will ever outrank him.

★ ★ ★ ★ ★ ★ ★ ★ ★

Franklin D. Roosevelt deservedly has a place
on U.S. currency. His image appears on the dime,
specifically, because of his role in establishing
the National Foundation for Infantile Paralysis
and its March of Dimes campaign.
The cause was particularly dear to him,
of course, because of his own paralysis from polio.

Richard M. Nixon never used the White House tennis courts.
His Secretary of the Interior, though, frequently did.
When the Secretary leaked a letter criticizing Nixon,
the president could have confronted him directly.
Instead, Nixon had the tennis courts removed.

Warren G. Harding was an incorrigible gambler. He even lost a set of White House china in one of his card games.

John Quincy Adams kept a strict morning routine.
Immediately after waking up, he would read several
Bible chapters before swimming in the Potomac.
Once, his admirable regimen backfired when someone
stole his clothes from the riverbank.
He had to ask a passerby to run to the White House
and bring him something else to wear.

"Wealth can only be accumulated
by the earnings of industry
and the savings of frugality."

JOHN TYLER

**Herbert Hoover never forgot
his humble beginnings as an orphan.
Long before he pursued politics,
his jobs included mining and picking
potato bugs off crops.
As president, he donated all of his
presidential salary to charity.**

"There is no dignity quite so impressive,
and no independence quite so important,
as living within your means."

CALVIN COOLIDGE

"If you live long enough, you'll make mistakes.
But if you learn from them, you'll be a better person.
It's how you handle adversity, not how it affects you.
The main thing is never quit, never quit, never quit."

BILL CLINTON

"Any man worth his salt will stick up for what he believes right,
but it takes a slightly better man to acknowledge instantly
and without reservation that he is in error."

ANDREW JACKSON

"My failures have been errors of judgment, not of intent."

ULYSSES S. GRANT, EIGHTH STATE OF THE UNION ADDRESS (1876)

"If I had permitted my failures, or what seemed to me at the time
a lack of success, to discourage me, I cannot see any way
in which I would ever have made progress."

CALVIN COOLIDGE

Andrew Jackson in the Battle of New Orleans (Everett Historical).

Illustration on the broadside engraved, printed, and sold by Paul Revere in 1770 (Everett Historical).

"The great enemy of the truth is very often not the lie—deliberate, contrived, and dishonest—but the myth—persistent, persuasive, and unrealistic."

JOHN F. KENNEDY

"Facts are stubborn things; and whatever may be our wishes, our inclination, or the dictates of our passions, they cannot alter the state of facts and evidence."

JOHN ADAMS IN THE BOSTON MASSACRE TRIAL, DECEMBER 4, 1770

"Truth is the glue that holds governments together. Compromise is the oil that makes governments go."

GERALD R. FORD

"How many legs does a dog have if you call the tail a leg? Four. Calling a tail a leg doesn't make it a leg."

ABRAHAM LINCOLN

"Above all, tell the truth."

GROVER CLEVELAND

ident Coolidge, Mrs. Coolidge, and canine visitor to the White House.

Michelle and Barack Obama join Joe Biden to watch the 2009 inauguration pa
(photo by Carol M. Highsm

"We did not come to fear the future.
We came here to shape it."

BARACK OBAMA

"Determine never to be idle.
No person will have occasion to complain of the want of time,
who never loses any. It is wonderful how much may be done,
if we are always doing."

THOMAS JEFFERSON, LETTER TO MARTHA JEFFERSON, MAY 5, 1787

"If you don't feel something strongly,
you're not going to achieve."

GEORGE W. BUSH

"Let us rather run the risk of
wearing out than rusting out."

THEODORE ROOSEVELT

"There is no pleasure in having nothing to do;
the fun is having lots to do and not doing it."

ANDREW JACKSON

Colonel Theodore Roosevelt leads the 1st United States Volunteer Cavalry in the charge up San Juan Hill during the Spanish-American War (Everett Historical).

"The credit belongs to the man who is actually in the arena, whose face is marred by dust and sweat and blood… who at the best knows in the end the triumph of high achievement, and who at the worst, if he fails, at least fails while daring greatly, so that his place shall never be with those cold and timid souls who neither know victory nor defeat."

THEODORE ROOSEVELT IN HIS "CITIZENSHIP IN A REPUBLIC" SPEECH, DELIVERED AT THE SORBONNE IN PARIS, FRANCE, ON APRIL 23, 1910

* * * * * * * * *

Andrew Johnson is the only president who never went to school.
He rose from humble beginnings as a tailor to become a senator,
the vice president, and ultimately the president. He took great pride in th[e]
democratic triumph, and, though not original to him, a maxim he mad[e]
famous in his speech at Logansport, Indiana, in 1864 was that
"if a man does not disgrace his profession, it never disgraces him."

"It is easier to do a job right
than to explain why you didn't."

MARTIN VAN BUREN

"Always give your best, never get discouraged,
never be petty; always remember, others may hate you.
Those who hate you don't win unless you hate them.
And then you destroy yourself."

RICHARD M. NIXON

"I always remember an epitaph which is in the cemetery
at Tombstone, Arizona. It says: 'Here lies Jack Williams.
He done his damnedest.' I think that is the greatest epitaph
a man can have—when he gives everything that is in him
to do the job he has before him. That is all you can ask of him
and that is what I have tried to do."

HARRY S. TRUMAN

"I have never in my life envied a human being
who led an easy life; I have envied a great many people
who led difficult lives and led them well."

THEODORE ROOSEVELT

★ ★ ★ ★ ★ ★ ★ ★ ★

"Your love of liberty—your respect for the laws—your habits of industry— and your practice of the moral and religious obligations, are the strongest claims to national and individual happiness."

GEORGE WASHINGTON IN A LETTER TO THE RESIDENTS OF BOSTON, OCTOBER 27, 1789

"Happiness lies in the joy of achievement and the thrill of creative effort."

FRANKLIN D. ROOSEVELT

"It is neither wealth nor splendor, but tranquility and occupation, which give happiness."

THOMAS JEFFERSON

"Far and away the best prize that life has to offer is the chance to work hard at work worth doing."

THEODORE ROOSEVELT

"A man who has never lost himself in a cause bigger than himself has missed one of life's mountaintop experiences. Only in losing himself does he find himself."

RICHARD M. NIXON

GIFT FOR THE GRANGERS

"You have to do your own growing
no matter how tall your grandfather was."

ABRAHAM LINCOLN

"Change will not come if we wait for some other person,
or if we wait for some other time. We are the ones we've
been waiting for. We are the change that we seek."

BARACK OBAMA

"The buck stops here."

HARRY S. TRUMAN
(HE MADE THIS HIS MAXIM, THOUGH HE DID NOT ORIGINATE THE PHRASE.)

"It should be the highest ambition of every American
to extend his views beyond himself, and to bear in mind
that his conduct will not only affect himself, his country,
and his immediate posterity; but that its influence may be
co-extensive with the world, and stamp political happiness
or misery on ages yet unborn."

GEORGE WASHINGTON IN HIS LETTER TO THE LEGISLATURE OF PENNSYLVANIA,
SEPTEMBER 5, 1789

"We grow great by dreams.
All big men are dreamers."

WOODROW WILSON

"Ambition is a commendable attribute
without which no man succeeds.
Only inconsiderate ambition imperils."

WARREN G. HARDING

"That's all a man can hope for during his lifetime—
to set an example—and when he is dead,
to be an inspiration for history."

WILLIAM MCKINLEY

"We need a spirit of community,
a sense that we are all in this together.
If we have no sense of community,
the American dream will wither."

BILL CLINTON

★ ★ ★ ★ ★ ★ ★ ★ ★

LITTLE DID YOU KNOW...

Though not a standout student, John F. Kennedy
was voted "most likely to succeed"
by his high school classmates.

★ FREEDOM ★

On our nation's most prized possession

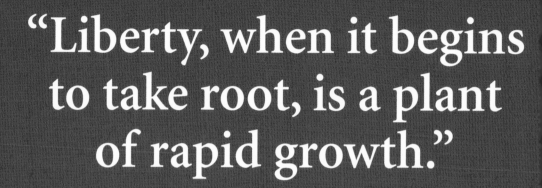

"Liberty, when it begins to take root, is a plant of rapid growth."

GEORGE WASHINGTON IN A LETTER TO JAMES MADISON, MARCH 2, 1788

★ ★ ★ ★ ★ ★ ★ ★ ★

"We know what works: Freedom works. We know what's right: Freedom is right."

GEORGE H. W. BUSH

Declaration of Independence by John Trumbull (1900).

"Freedom is the recognition that no single person,
no single authority or government, has a monopoly
on the truth, but that every individual life is infinitely precious,
that every one of us put in this world has been put there for a
reason and has something to offer."

RONALD REAGAN

"Our American values are not luxuries but necessities—
not the salt in our bread, but the bread itself. Our common vision
of a free and just society is our greatest source of cohesion at home a
strength abroad—greater than the bounty of our material blessings

JIMMY CARTER, FAREWELL ADDRESS, JANUARY 14, 1981

"Citizens by birth or choice of a common country,
that country has a right to concentrate your affections.
The name of American, which belongs to you, in your national
capacity, must always exalt the just pride of Patriotism,
more than any appellation derived from local discriminations."

GEORGE WASHINGTON, FAREWELL ADDRESS, SEPTEMBER 19, 1796

"The value of liberty was thus enhanced in our estimation by the difficulty of its attainment."

GEORGE WASHINGTON IN A LETTER TO THE PEOPLE OF SOUTH CAROLINA, 1790

★ ★ ★

"The American continents,
by the free and independent condition
which they have assumed and maintain,
are henceforth not to be considered as
subjects for future colonization by any
European powers."

JAMES MONROE, SEVENTH ANNUAL MESSAGE
("THE MONROE DOCTRINE"), DECEMBER 2, 1823

We the People

of the United States, in order to form a more perfect Union, establish Justice, insure domestic Tranquility, provide for the common defence, promote the general Welfare, and secure the Blessings of Liberty to ourselves and our Posterity, do ordain and establish this Constitution for the United States of America.

Article I

Section 1. All legislative Powers herein granted shall be vested in a Congress of the United States, which shall consist of a Senate and House of Representatives.

Section 2. The House of Representatives shall be composed of Members chosen every second Year by the People of the several States, and the Electors in each State shall have the Qualifications requisite for Electors of the most numerous Branch of the State Legislature.

No Person shall be a Representative who shall not have attained to the Age of twenty five Years, and been seven Years a Citizen of the United States, and who shall not, when elected, be an Inhabitant of that State in which he shall be chosen.

Representatives and direct Taxes shall be apportioned among the several States which may be included within this Union, according to their respective Numbers, which shall be determined by adding to the whole Number of free Persons, including those bound to Service for a Term of Years, and excluding Indians not taxed, three fifths of all other Persons. The actual Enumeration shall be made within three Years after the first Meeting of the Congress of the United States, and within every subsequent Term of ten Years, in such Manner as they shall by Law direct. The Number of Representatives shall not exceed one for every thirty Thousand, but each State shall have at Least one Representative; and until such enumeration shall be made, the State of New Hampshire shall be entitled to chuse three, Massachusetts eight, Rhode-Island and Providence Plantations one, Connecticut five, New-York six, New Jersey four, Pennsylvania eight, Delaware one, Maryland six, Virginia ten, North Carolina five, South Carolina five, and Georgia three.

When vacancies happen in the Representation from any State, the Executive Authority thereof shall issue Writs of Election to fill such Vacancies.

The House of Representatives shall chuse their Speaker and other Officers; and shall have the sole Power of Impeachment.

Section 3. The Senate of the United States shall be composed of two Senators from each State, chosen by the Legislature thereof, for six Years; and each Senator shall have one Vote.

Immediately after they shall be assembled in Consequence of the first Election, they shall be divided as equally as may be into three Classes. The Seats of the Senators of the first Class shall be vacated at the Expiration of the second Year, of the second Class at the Expiration of the fourth Year, and of the third Class at the Expiration of the sixth Year, so that one third may be chosen every second Year; and if Vacancies happen by Resignation, or otherwise, during the Recess of the Legislature of any State, the Executive thereof may make temporary Appointments until the next Meeting of the Legislature, which shall then fill such Vacancies.

No Person shall be a Senator who shall not have attained to the Age of thirty Years, and been nine Years a Citizen of the United States, and who shall not, when elected, be an Inhabitant of that State for which he shall be chosen.

The Vice President of the United States shall be President of the Senate, but shall have no Vote, unless they be equally divided.

The Senate shall chuse their other Officers, and also a President pro tempore, in the Absence of the Vice President, or when he shall exercise the Office of President of the United States.

The Senate shall have the sole Power to try all Impeachments. When sitting for that Purpose, they shall be on Oath or Affirmation. When the President of the United States is tried, the Chief Justice shall preside: And no Person shall be convicted without the Concurrence of two thirds of the Members present.

Judgment in Cases of Impeachment shall not extend further than to removal from Office, and disqualification to hold and enjoy any Office of honor, Trust or Profit under the United States: but the Party convicted shall nevertheless be liable and subject to Indictment, Trial, Judgment and Punishment, according to Law.

Section 4. The Times, Places and Manner of holding Elections for Senators and Representatives, shall be prescribed in each State by the Legislature thereof; but the Congress may at any time by Law make or alter such Regulations, except as to the Places of chusing Senators.

The Congress shall assemble at least once in every Year, and such Meeting shall be on the first Monday in December, unless they shall by Law appoint a different Day.

Section 5. Each House shall be the Judge of the Elections, Returns and Qualifications of its own Members, and a Majority of each shall constitute a Quorum to do Business; but a smaller Number may adjourn from day to day, and may be authorized to compel the Attendance of absent Members, in such Manner, and under such Penalties as each House may provide.

Each House may determine the Rules of its Proceedings, punish its Members for disorderly Behaviour, and, with the Concurrence of two thirds, expel a Member.

Each House shall keep a Journal of its Proceedings, and from time to time publish the same, excepting such Parts as may in their Judgment require Secrecy; and the Yeas and Nays of the Members of either House on any question shall, at the Desire of one fifth of those Present, be entered on the Journal.

Neither House, during the Session of Congress, shall, without the Consent of the other, adjourn for more than three days, nor to any other Place than that in which the two Houses shall be sitting.

Section 6. The Senators and Representatives shall receive a Compensation for their Services, to be ascertained by Law, and paid out of the Treasury of the United States. They shall in all Cases, except Treason, Felony and Breach of the Peace, be privileged from Arrest during their Attendance at the Session of their respective Houses, and in going to and returning from the same; and for any Speech or Debate in either House, they shall not be questioned in any other Place.

No Senator or Representative shall, during the Time for which he was elected, be appointed to any civil Office under the Authority of the United States, which shall have been created, or the Emoluments whereof shall have been encreased during such time; and no Person holding any Office under the United States, shall be a Member of either House during his Continuance in Office.

"But a Constitution of Government
once changed from Freedom,
can never be restored.
Liberty, once lost, is lost forever."

JOHN ADAMS IN A LETTER TO ABIGAIL ADAMS, JULY 17, 1775

"The Constitution is the bedrock of all our freedoms;
guard and cherish it; keep honor and order
in your own house; and the republic will endure."

GERALD R. FORD

★ ★ ★ ★ ★ ★ ★ ★ ★

"There is nothing stable but Heaven and the Constitution."

JAMES BUCHANAN

"The more I study [the Constitution] the more I have come to admire it, realizing that no other document devised by the hand of man ever brought so much progress and happiness to humanity."

CALVIN COOLIDGE

"The storm of frenzy and faction must inevitably dash itself in vain against the unshaken rock of the Constitution."

FRANKLIN PIERCE

Warren G. Harding literally saved the Constitution.
Before his intervention, it was crumbling away
in State Department files. Harding had it
put in a protective glass case
for future generations to see.

★ ★ ★ ★ ★ ★ ★ ★ ★ ★

"If slavery is not wrong, nothing is wrong."

ABRAHAM LINCOLN, IN A LETTER TO ALBERT HODGES,
EDITOR OF KENTUCKY'S *FRANKFORT COMMONWEALTH*, APRIL 4, 1864

Though unwilling to take political action to end slavery, **James Buchanan** would buy slaves in Washington, D.C., with his own money to set them free in Northern states.

"I believe there are more instances of the abridgement
of the freedom of the people by gradual and silent encroachments
of those in power than by violent and sudden usurpations."

JAMES MADISON

"Whenever I hear anyone arguing for slavery,
I feel a strong impulse to see it tried on him personally."

ABRAHAM LINCOLN

An illustration questioning the effectiveness of the Emancipation Proclamation, published in *Harper's Weekly* in 1867.

★ ★ ★ ★ ★ ★ ★ ★ ★

Lyndon B. Johnson and Lady Bird Johnson hosted a
Festival of the Arts at the White House in 1965.
With a star-studded guest list of luminary
American artists, it was the first event of its kind.
Sarah Vaughan, an award-winning jazz singer,
performed to thunderous applause. Afterward,
a White House staffer found Vaughan crying in her dressing
room. When the staffer asked what was wrong,
Vaughan answered, "Nothing is the matter.
It's just that twenty years ago when I came to Washington,
I couldn't even get a hotel room,
and tonight I sang for the president of the United States
in the White House—and then, he asked me to dance
with him. It is more than I can stand!"

★ ★ ★ ★ ★ ★ ★ ★ ★

"We need not fear the expression of ideas— we do need to fear their suppression."

HARRY S. TRUMAN, SPEECH ON THE VETO OF THE
MCCARRAN INTERNAL SECURITY ACT, SEPTEMBER 22, 1950

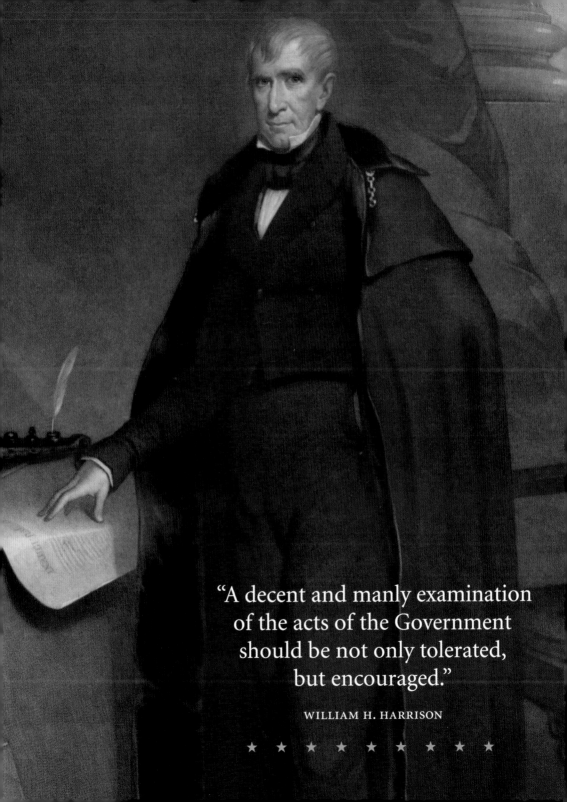

"A decent and manly examination of the acts of the Government should be not only tolerated, but encouraged."

WILLIAM H. HARRISON

★ ★ ★ ★ ★ ★ ★ ★ ★ ★ ★

"Public opinion sets bounds to every government,
and is the real sovereign in every free one."

JAMES MADISON IN A *NATIONAL GAZETTE* ESSAY, FEBRUARY 2, 1792

"Absolute freedom of the press
to discuss public questions is
a foundation stone of American liberty."

HERBERT HOOVER

"To announce that there must be no criticism of the president,
or that we are to stand by the president, right or wrong,
is not only unpatriotic and servile,
but is morally treasonable to the American public."

THEODORE ROOSEVELT

"If we cannot end now our differences,
at least we can help make
the world safe for diversity."

JOHN F. KENNEDY

"The legitimate powers of government
extend to such acts only as are injurious to others.
But it does me no injury for my neighbor
to say there are twenty gods, or no god.
It neither picks my pocket nor breaks my leg."

THOMAS JEFFERSON IN "NOTES ON THE STATE OF VIRGINIA, QUERY 17," 1781

LITTLE DID YOU KNOW...

Barack Obama had perhaps the most multicultural
childhood of any president—besides his diverse heritage
with a Kenyan father and Euro-American mother,
he spent the majority of his young years between
Hawaii and Indonesia.

"The separation of church and state is a source of strength, but the conscience of our nation does not call for separation between men of state and faith in the Supreme Being."

LYNDON B. JOHNSON

"The spirit of resistance to government is so valuable on certain occasions, that I wish it to be always kept alive. It will often be exercised when wrong, but better so than not to be exercised at all. I like a little rebellion now and then. It is like a storm in the atmosphere."

THOMAS JEFFERSON IN A LETTER TO ABIGAIL ADAMS, FEBRUARY 22, 1787

"We must not then depend alone upon the love of liberty in the soul of man for its preservation."

JOHN ADAMS TO SAMUEL ADAMS, OCTOBER 18, 1790

"I would rather belong to a poor nation that was free than to a rich nation that had ceased to be in love with liberty."

WOODROW WILSON

Sheet music cover, 1919.

"What spectacle can be more edifying or more seasonable, than that of Liberty and Learning, each leaning on the other for their mutual & surest support?"

JAMES MADISON IN A LETTER TO W. T. BARRY, AUGUST 4, 1822

"Children should be educated and instructed in the principles of freedom."

JOHN ADAMS IN HIS *A DEFENCE OF THE CONSTITUTIONS OF GOVERNMENT OF THE UNITED STATES OF AMERICA, 1787*

"Enlighten the people, generally, and tyranny and oppressions of body and mind will vanish like spirits at the dawn of day."

THOMAS JEFFERSON, LETTER TO PIERRE SAMUEL DUPONT DE NEMOURS, APRIL 24, 1816

"The preservation of the sacred fire of liberty,
and the destiny of the republican model of government,
are justly considered deeply, perhaps as finally,
staked, on the experiment entrusted
to the hands of the American people."

GEORGE WASHINGTON, FIRST INAUGURAL ADDRESS, APRIL 30, 1789

"Let us not, in cowering and foolish fear,
throw away the ideals which are the
fundamental basis of our free society...."

HARRY S. TRUMAN, SPEECH ON THE VETO OF THE
MCCARRAN INTERNAL SECURITY ACT, SEPTEMBER 22, 1950

"I can never consent to being dictated to."

JOHN TYLER

★ ★ ★ ★ ★ ★ ★ ★ ★

"Men may die, but the fabrics
of our free institutions remain unshaken."

CHESTER A. ARTHUR

"America is best described by one word, freedom."

DWIGHT D. EISENHOWER

"The cost of freedom is always high,
but Americans have always paid it.
And one path we shall never choose,
and that is the path of surrender,
or submission."

JOHN F. KENNEDY

★ ★ ★ ★ ★ ★ ★ ★ ★

Woodrow Wilson.

★QUIPS★

The lighter side of our leaders

"An economist is someone who sees something happen in practice and wonders if it'd work in theory."

RONALD REAGAN

"Washington is a city of Southern efficiency and Northern charm."

JOHN F. KENNEDY

"Golf is an ineffectual attempt
to put an elusive ball into an obscure hole
with implements ill-adapted to the purpose."

WOODROW WILSON

President Warren G. Harding playing golf.

"If you could kick the person in the pant responsible for most of your trouble, you wouldn't sit for a month."

THEODORE ROOSEVELT

"The truth will set you free,
but first it will make you miserable."

JAMES A. GARFIELD

"I have never been hurt
by anything I didn't say."

CALVIN COOLIDGE

"If you want to make enemies,
try to change something."

WOODROW WILSON

"About the time we think we can make ends meet,
somebody moves the ends."

HERBERT HOOVER

★ ★ ★ ★ ★ ★ ★ ★ ★

Benjamin Harrison was the first president
to have electricity in the White House,
but he was so afraid of electrocution that he
would never touch the light switches himself.

★ ★ ★ ★ ★ ★ ★ ★ ★

James Madison was quite the fashion-forward president.
He was the first to show his own hair in public, rather than a wig,
and led the switch from knee breeches to full-length pants.

"A man is known by the company he keeps,
and also by the company from which he is kept out."

GROVER CLEVELAND

"He can compress the most words into the smallest ideas
better than any man I ever met."

ABRAHAM LINCOLN

"Labor disgraces no man;
unfortunately, you occasionally find
men who disgrace labor."

ULYSSES S. GRANT

"Never murder a man who is committing suicide."

**WOODROW WILSON,
BORROWING FROM A PRECEPT COMMONLY ATTRIBUTED TO NAPOLEON**

"I can't talk about my opponent the way I would like to sometimes,
because I try to think that I am a Christian."

FRANKLIN D. ROOSEVELT, FINAL PRESIDENTIAL CAMPAIGN, 1944

"When the president does it,
that means it's not illegal."

RICHARD M. NIXON, 1977 INTERVIEW WITH DAVID FROST

Jimmy Carter was attacked by a swimming rabbit.
The press had a field day when they got a hold
of the story—one cartoon parodied the *Jaws* poster
and captioned the image "PAWS."

"I have opinions of my own—strong opinions—
but I don't always agree with them."

GEORGE W. BUSH

James K. Polk was every bit as distrustful of banks
in his private life as he proclaimed himself to be politically.
He refused to use paper money, stashing gold and silver
in a trunk under his bed and even carrying bags
of coins with him during the day.

Warsaw, 1946

"Well, not at the time.
But I was scared stiff three weeks later
when I got around to reading
the newspaper accounts."

DWIGHT D. EISENHOWER,
WHEN ASKED IF HE'D BEEN AFRAID DURING THE BATTLE OF THE BULGE

"It's true hard work never killed anybody,
but I figure, why take the chance?"

RONALD REAGAN

According to legend, **John Tyler** once sent his son Bob to specially
commission a train for his travel. The railroad superintendent refused,
saying that he didn't run trains by request, not even for the president.
When Bob pointed out that there had been a train specifically
for the funeral of Tyler's predecessor, William H. Harrison,
the superintendent replied, "Yes, and if you will bring your father
here in that shape, you shall have the best train on the road!"

★ ★ ★ ★ ★ ★ ★ ★ ★

"I'm comfortable playing
[golf with Ford], as long as my caddie
and I have the same blood type."

GEORGE H. W. BUSH

"I want a one-armed economist
so that the guy could never make a statement
and then say 'on the other hand…'"

HARRY S. TRUMAN

"It has been my experience
that folks who have no vices
generally have very few virtues."

ABRAHAM LINCOLN

Ronald Reagan put his film experience to use when running against Jimmy Carter. After a debate between the two, Reagan walked across the stage to shake Carter's hand. Maybe this was a gesture of goodwill. Or maybe Reagan wanted to show that he was clearly the taller— and more presidential—of the candidates.

Zachary Taylor liked his dish of hominy,
but only when made with sweet corn.
His horse Claybank shared this taste,
which Taylor used to his advantage.
When on campaign as a general, he would
let his horse sniff around the bags of usually
musty corn brought in to feed the army until
Claybank chomped down on a bag of good corn.
The general would then order that the horse
be sent to the stable, but since it had chewed
a hole in the corn bag, they might as well take
the grain and make a batch of hominy.

"I have left orders to be awakened at any time
in case of national emergency—
even if I'm in a cabinet meeting."

RONALD REAGAN

"I know there are some Republicans and some Democrats
who say that they have now developed a wonderful
arrangement in Washington. The Congress is Democratic
and the president is Republican and nothing happens,
and isn't it wonderful?"

JOHN F. KENNEDY

"Combining the Bureau of Alcohol, Tobacco, and Firearms
with both the Bureau of Fisheries and the Interstate Truckin
Commission. We're going to call it the Department of Guys.

BILL CLINTON IN 1995, ON WAYS THE GOVERNMENT CAN SAVE MONEY

"One way to make sure crime doesn't pay
would be to let the government run it."

RONALD REAGAN

"We... declared our independence 200 years ago, and we are not about to lose it now to paper shufflers and computers."

GERALD R. FORD

"Politics is not a bad profession.
If you succeed, there are many rewards.
If you disgrace yourself,
you can always write a book."

RONALD REAGAN

"I just received the following wire
from my generous daddy: 'Dear Jack,
Don't buy a single vote more than is necessary.
I'll be damned if I'm going to pay for a landslide.'"

JOHN F. KENNEDY

"If one morning I walked on top of
the water across the Potomac River,
the headline that afternoon would read:
'President Can't Swim.'"

LYNDON B. JOHNSON

"There are advantages
to being elected president.
The day after I was elected,
I had my high school grades
classified Top Secret."

RONALD REAGAN

The Democratic Party refused to renominate
Franklin Pierce after his first term.
When asked what a president should do upon leaving office,
he replied, "There's nothing left… but to get drunk."

"Being president is like running a cemetery:
you've got a lot of people under you
and nobody's listening."

BILL CLINTON

"Being a president is like being
a jackass in a hailstorm. There's nothing to do
but stand there and take it."

LYNDON B. JOHNSON

"I sit here all day trying to persuade people
to do the things they ought to have the sense
to do without my persuading them.
That's all the powers of the president amount to."

HARRY S. TRUMAN

Engraving of Ulysses S. Grant by William Sartain (18

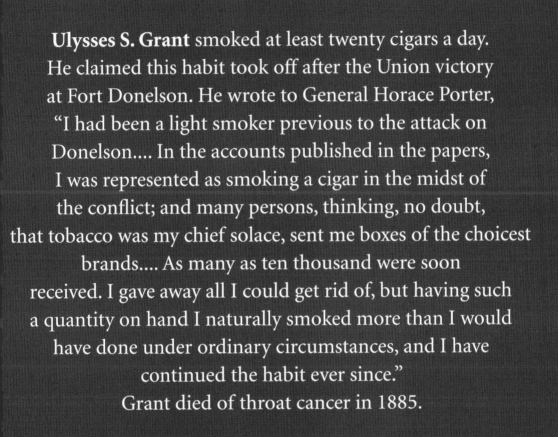

Ulysses S. Grant smoked at least twenty cigars a day.
He claimed this habit took off after the Union victory
at Fort Donelson. He wrote to General Horace Porter,
"I had been a light smoker previous to the attack on
Donelson.... In the accounts published in the papers,
I was represented as smoking a cigar in the midst of
the conflict; and many persons, thinking, no doubt,
that tobacco was my chief solace, sent me boxes of the choicest
brands.... As many as ten thousand were soon
received. I gave away all I could get rid of, but having such
a quantity on hand I naturally smoked more than I would
have done under ordinary circumstances, and I have
continued the habit ever since."
Grant died of throat cancer in 1885.

Teddy Jr. and Eli Yale.

Theodore Roosevelt and his six children loved animals.
Their pets included a bear, a herd of guinea pigs, a hyena,
a barn owl, and a snake. Once, young Quentin Roosevelt thought
he'd add some more snakes to the menagerie, so he bought four more
and brought them to see his father. The president was in a
cabinet meeting at the time. The important government officials smiled
indulgently at the boy wanting to see his dad. However, when
Quentin revealed the snakes, dropping them on the table,
the grown men promptly scattered.

"The pay is good and I can walk to work."

JOHN F. KENNEDY

"You have to stand every day three or four hours of visitors. Nine-tenths of them want something they ought not to have. f you keep dead still they will run down in three or four minutes. If you even cough or smile they will start up all over again."

CALVIN COOLIDGE

LITTLE DID YOU KNOW...

Twenty-four wagons' worth of junk left by presidents and their families were carted away from the White House after Chester A. Arthur ordered its total cleaning, repairing, and refurbishment. Lincoln's pants and a hat that belonged to John Quincy Adams were among the items auctioned off.

"I Pray Heaven to Bestow The Best of Blessing on THIS HOUSE [the White House], and on ALL that shall hereafter Inhabit it. May none but Honest and Wise Men ever rule under This Roof!"

JOHN ADAMS

IN A LETTER TO HIS WIFE ABIGAIL, NOVEMBER 2, 1800. FRANKLIN D. ROOSEVELT HAD THIS LETTERED IN GOLD IN THE MARBLE OVER THE FIREPLACE IN THE STATE DINING ROOM OF THE WHITE HOUSE.

Andrew Jackson really liked cheese, and the public was well aware. In a fit of patriotic support, one New York dairy farmer sent the president a 1,400-pound wheel of cheddar. Though initially stumped by what to do with such a mound of dairy, Jackson soon struck on the idea to bring the cheese out at his final White House public reception. His open parties were so well attended that within two hours the guests had devoured every sign of the cheese—except for its smell, which lingered in the White House, much to the annoyance of Jackson's successor.

Benjamin Franklin, John Adams, and Thomas Jefferson writing the Declaration of Independence, 17
From a 1909 lithograph by Wolf &

★ GOVERNANCE ★

On leadership, how government should be,
the dangers and burdens of power,
and the presidency itself

"The care of human life and happiness,
and not their destruction, is the first and only
legitimate object of good government."

THOMAS JEFFERSON IN A LETTER TO THE REPUBLICAN CITIZENS
OF WASHINGTON COUNTY, MARYLAND, MARCH 31, 1809

"The problem to be solved is,
not what form of Government is perfect,
but which of the forms is least imperfect."

JAMES MADISON IN A LETTER TO WILLIAM COGSWELL, MARCH 10, 1834

"If government is to serve any purpose,
it is to do for others what they are unable
to do for themselves."

LYNDON B. JOHNSON

"That government is best which governs the least."

THOMAS JEFFERSON

"On the farms, in the large metropolitan areas, in the smaller cities, and in the villages, millions of our citizens cherish the hope that their old standards of living and of thought have not gone forever. Those millions cannot and shall not hope in vain. I pledge you, I pledge myself, to a new deal for the American people."

FRANKLIN D. ROOSEVELT,
ACCEPTING THE DEMOCRATIC NOMINATION FOR PRESIDENT, 1933

"Internal improvement and the diffusion of knowledge, so far as they can be promoted by the constitutional acts of the Federal Government, are of high importance."

ANDREW JACKSON

"The ballot box is the surest arbiter of disputes among freemen."

JAMES BUCHANAN

"Unlike any other nation, here the people rule, and their will is the supreme law. It is sometimes sneeringly said by those who do not like free government, that here we count heads. True, heads are counted, but brains also."

WILLIAM MCKINLEY

"As I would not be a slave, so I would not be a master. This expresses my idea of democracy."

ABRAHAM LINCOLN

"The best way to enhance freedom in other lands is to demonstrate here that our democratic system is worthy of emulation."

JIMMY CARTER

"When we got into office,
the thing that surprised me most
was to find that things were just as bad
as we'd been saying they were."

JOHN F. KENNEDY

"He serves his party best who serves the country best."

RUTHERFORD B. HAYES

"Although in our country the Chief Magistrate
must almost of necessity be chosen by a party and stand
pledged to its principles and measures, yet in his official
action he should not be the President of a party only,
but of the whole people of the United States."

JAMES K. POLK

William H. Harrison campaign headquarters in Philadelphia, 1840 (Everett Historical).

"The great can protect themselves,
but the poor and humble require
the arm and shield of the law."

ANDREW JACKSON, 1821

"There is no calamity which a great nation
can invite which equals that which follows
a supine submission to wrong and injustice."

GROVER CLEVELAND

"The best and only safe road to honor,
glory, and true dignity is justice."

GEORGE WASHINGTON IN A LETTER TO MARQUIS DE LAFAYETTE, SEPTEMBER 30, 1779

"Let justice be done though
the heavens should fall."

JOHN ADAMS IN A LETTER TO ELBRIDGE GERRY, DECEMBER 5, 1777

"There is nothing wrong with America that the faith, love of freedom, intelligence, and energy of her citizens cannot cure."

DWIGHT D. EISENHOWER

"Knowledge is, in every country, the surest basis of public happiness."

GEORGE WASHINGTON IN HIS FIRST ANNUAL MESSAGE, JANUARY 8, 1790

"No one more sincerely wishes the spread of information among mankind than I do, and none has greater confidence in its effect towards supporting free and good government."

THOMAS JEFFERSON IN A LETTER TO TRUSTEES FOR THE LOTTERY OF EAST TENNESSEE COLLEGE, MAY 6, 1810

Detail from an engraving of George Washington by H. S. Sadd, 1844.

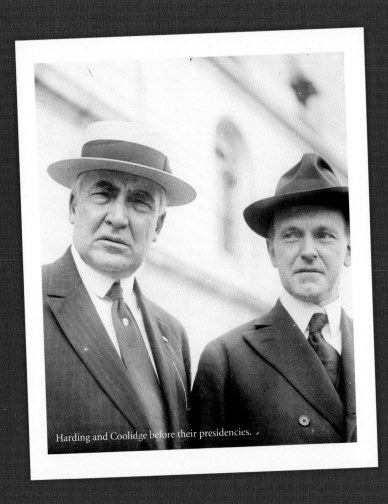

Harding and Coolidge before their presidencies.

The then vice president **Calvin Coolidge** was visiting his childhood hom
in Vermont when President Harding died. Coolidge's father
woke him with the news, telling him that he was now the president.
A notary public, the elder Mr. Coolidge then swore his son
into office and was the first to call him "Mr. President."
The new president then went back to bed.

"For myself, therefore, I desire to declare that the
principle that will govern me in the high duty to which
my country calls me is a strict adherence to the letter
and spirit of the Constitution as it was designed
by those who framed it."

MARTIN VAN BUREN

"The man who can look upon a crisis
without being willing to offer himself upon the altar
of his country is not for public trust."

MILLARD FILLMORE

"Honest conviction is my courage;
the Constitution is my guide."

ANDREW JOHNSON

"Do what you can with what
you have, where you are."

THEODORE ROOSEVELT

★ ★ ★ ★ ★ ★ ★ ★ ★

"The office in such times as these makes its incumbent a repairman behind a dike. No sooner is one leak plugged up than it is necessary to dash over and stop another that has broken out. There is no end to it."

HERBERT HOOVER

"No president has ever enjoyed himself as much as I."

THEODORE ROOSEVELT

"The intoxication of power rapidly sobers off in the knowledge of its restrictions and under the prompt reminder of an ever-present and not always considerate press, as well as the kindly suggestions that not infrequently come from Congress."

WILLIAM H. TAFT

"A good leader
can't get too far ahead
of his followers."

FRANKLIN D. ROOSEVELT

★ ★ ★ ★ ★ ★ ★ ★

"I learned that a great man is a man
who has the ability to get other people to do
what they don't want to do and like it."

HARRY S. TRUMAN

"I'm a success today because I had a friend
who believed in me and I didn't have
the heart to let him down."

ABRAHAM LINCOLN

"I have a different vision of leadership.
A leader is someone who brings people together."

GEORGE W. BUSH

"Whatever the result may be,
I shall carry to my grave the consciousness that
I at least meant well for my country."

JAMES BUCHANAN

"I never saw a pessimistic general win a battle."

DWIGHT D. EISENHOWER

> "I am heartily rejoiced that my term
> is so near its close. I will soon cease to be
> a servant and will become a sovereign."

JAMES K. POLK

LITTLE DID YOU KNOW...

When the founders voted on who should head the committee
for drafting the Declaration of Independence, John Adams
and Thomas Jefferson got the highest number of votes.
As Adams told it, Jefferson first tried to propose that Adams
be the one to write the document, but the latter refused, and
instead delegated the task back to Jefferson with many compliments.
Adams said, "I am obnoxious, suspected, and unpopular.
You are very much otherwise.... [And] you can write ten times better
than I can." Jefferson accepted, and Adams declared, very much
the committee chair, "Very well. When you have drawn it up,
we will have a meeting."

Mount Vernon.

"I can truly say I had rather be at Mount Vernon with a friend or two about me, than to be attended at the Seat of Government by the Officers of State and the Representatives of every Power in Europe."

GEORGE WASHINGTON IN A LETTER TO DAVID STUART, JUNE 15, 1790

"The truth is that all men having power ought to be mistrusted."

JAMES MADISON

"How difficult it has been for mankind, in all ages and countries, to preserve their dearest rights and best privileges, impelled as it were by an irresistible fate of despotism."

JAMES MONROE, SPEECH IN THE VIRGINIA RATIFYING CONVENTION, JUNE 10, 1788

"There is no grievance that is a fit object of redress by mob law."

ABRAHAM LINCOLN, ADDRESS BEFORE THE YOUNG MEN'S LYCEUM OF SPRINGFIELD, ILLINOIS, JANUARY 27, 1838

In 1865, six-year-old Teddy Roosevelt
and his brother, Elliott,
future father of Eleanor Roosevelt,
watched the funeral procession
of Abraham Lincoln from a
second-story window in New York City.

Bill Clinton was a delegate in the American Legion's Boys Nation program, giving him the chance to meet **President Kennedy** at a White House reception. The moment he shook the president's hand was the moment he decided that he too would go into politics.

"He shows all the backbone
of a chocolate éclair."

THEODORE ROOSEVELT ON PREDECESSOR WILLIAM MCKINLEY

"A man whose soul might be turned wrong side outward, without discovering a blemish to the world."

THOMAS JEFFERSON ON JAMES MADISON

"One of the pillars and ornaments of his country and of his age… His time on Earth was short, yet he died full of years and of glory…. He has improved his own condition by improving that of his country and his kind."

JOHN QUINCY ADAMS IN HIS EULOGY TO JAMES MADISON

"I think this is the most extraordinary collection of talent, of human knowledge, that has ever been gathered together at the White House, with the possible exception of when Thomas Jefferson dined alone."

JOHN F. KENNEDY AT A WHITE HOUSE DINNER
HONORING NOBEL PRIZE WINNERS OF THE WESTERN HEMISPHERE

★ NATION ★

On the creation, preservation, and legacy of our country

"Our country abounds in the necessaries,
the arts, and the comforts of life."

JAMES MADISON, MARCH 4, 1813

"Fear is the foundation of most governments;
but it is so sordid and brutal a passion, and renders men
in whose breasts it predominates so stupid and miserable,
that Americans will not be likely to approve of any
political institution which is founded on it."

JOHN ADAMS, "THOUGHTS ON GOVERNMENT," 1776

"No other people have a government
more worthy of their respect and love
or a land so magnificent in extent...."

BENJAMIN HARRISON

"We are a nation that has a government—
not the other way around.
And that makes us special among the
nations of the Earth."

RONALD REAGAN

"The United States is the best and fairest and most decent nation on the face of the Earth."

GEORGE H. W. BUSH

★ ★ ★ ★ ★ ★ ★ ★ ★

American Progress by John Gast (1872).

"Four score and seven years ago our fathers
brought forth on this continent a new nation,
conceived in liberty and dedicated to the proposition
that all men are created equal."

ABRAHAM LINCOLN, GETTYSBURG ADDRESS, NOVEMBER 19, 1863

"America did not invent human rights.
In a very real sense, it is the other way around.
Human rights invented America."

JIMMY CARTER

"The deliberate union of so great and various a people
in such a place, is without all partiality or prejudice,
if not the greatest exertion of human understanding,
the greatest single effort of national deliberation
that the world has ever seen."

JOHN ADAMS, QUOTED IN A LETTER FROM RUFUS KING
TO THEOPHILUS PARSONS, FEBRUARY 20, 1788

"The promise of America is a simple promise:
every person shall share in the blessings of this land.
And they shall share on the basis of their merits
as a person. They shall not be judged by their color
or by their beliefs, or by their religion, or by where they
were born, or the neighborhood in which they live."

LYNDON B. JOHNSON

"It will be worthy of a free, enlightened, and, at no distant period, a great Nation, to give to mankind the magnanimous and too novel example of a People always guided by an exalted justice and benevolence."

GEORGE WASHINGTON, FAREWELL ADDRESS, SEPTEMBER 19, 1796

"National honor is a national property of the highest value."

JAMES MONROE

"The American, by nature, is optimistic. He is experimental, an inventor, and a builder who builds best when called upon to build greatly."

JOHN F. KENNEDY

"Some people call me an idealist.
Well, that is the way I know am an American.
America is the only idealistic nation
in the world."

WOODROW WILSON

"The foundations of our national policy will be laid
in the pure and immutable principles of private morality,
and the preeminence of free government be exemplified
by all the attributes which can win the affections of its citizens,
and command the respect of the world."

GEORGE WASHINGTON, FIRST INAUGURAL ADDRESS, APRIL 30, 1789

"The example of changing a constitution
by assembling the wise men of the state,
instead of assembling armies, will be worth
as much to the world as the former examples
we had given them."

THOMAS JEFFERSON, LETTER TO DAVID HUMPHREYS, MARCH 18, 1789

"Objects of the most stupendous magnitude,
and measures in which the lives and liberties
of millions yet unborn are intimately interested,
are now before us. We are in the very midst of
a revolution the most complete, unexpected, and
remarkable of any in the history of nations."

JOHN ADAMS, LETTER TO WILLIAM CUSHING, JUNE 9, 1776

"For more than half a century,
during which kingdoms and empires have fallen,
this Union has stood unshaken.
The patriots who formed it have long since
descended to the grave; yet still it remains,
the proudest monument to their memory."

ZACHARY TAYLOR

"We cannot overestimate the fervent love of liberty, the intelligent courage, and the sum of common sense with which our fathers made the great experiment of self-government."

JAMES A. GARFIELD

"America, with the same voice which spoke herself into existence as a nation, proclaimed to mankind the inextinguishable rights of human nature, and the only lawful foundations of government."

JOHN QUINCY ADAMS

"As Americans, we can take enormous pride in the fact that courage has been inspired by our own struggle for freedom, by the tradition of democratic law secured by our forefathers and enshrined in our Constitution."

BARACK OBAMA

★ ★ ★ ★ ★ ★ ★

LITTLE DID YOU KNOW...

Martin Van Buren was the first president born an American citizen.
The seven before him were all British citizens.

"I tread in the footsteps of illustrious men,
whose superiors it is our happiness
to believe are not found on the
executive calendar of any country."

MARTIN VAN BUREN

When **Andrew Jackson** was president, a citizen asked that he give a postmaster job to a veteran who had lost his leg and was struggling to feed his family. When the man told Jackson that the soldier had voted against him, the president replied, "If he lost a leg fighting for his country, that is vote enough for me."

"Ask not what your country can do for you—
ask what you can do for your country."

JOHN F. KENNEDY, INAUGURAL ADDRESS, JANUARY 20, 1961

"It is the duty of a citizen
not only to observe the law
but to let it be known that
he is opposed to its violation."

CALVIN COOLIDGE

"To some generations much is given.
Of other generations much is asked.
This generation of Americans has a
rendezvous with destiny."

FRANKLIN D. ROOSEVELT,
ADDRESS TO THE DEMOCRATIC NATIONAL CONVENTION, 1936

★ ★ ★ ★ ★ ★ ★ ★

"The test of our progress is not whether we add more to the abundance of those who have too much; it is whether we provide enough for those who have too little."

FRANKLIN D. ROOSEVELT, SECOND INAUGURAL ADDRESS, 1937

"No country upon Earth ever had it more in its power
to attain these blessings than United America.
Wondrously strange, then, and much to be regretted indeed
would it be, were we to neglect the means and to
depart from the road which Providence has pointed us
to so plainly; I cannot believe it will ever come to pass."

GEORGE WASHINGTON, LETTER TO BENJAMIN LINCOLN, JUNE 29, 1788

"If anyone tells you that America's
best days are behind her,
they're looking the wrong way."

GEORGE H. W. BUSH

"A splendid storehouse of integrity and freedom
has been bequeathed to us by our forefathers.
In this day of confusion, of peril to liberty,
our high duty is to see that this storehouse
is not robbed of its contents."

HERBERT HOOVER

Yankee Doodle 1776 by Archibald M. Willard, ca. 1876

"I voted against Lincoln. I spoke against him.
I spent my money to defeat him.
But still I love my country."

ANDREW JOHNSON,
WHEN HE REFUSED TO ABANDON HIS POSITION AS TENNESSEE SENATOR
EVEN THOUGH EVERY OTHER SOUTHERN SENATOR HAD LEFT

"America united with a handful of troops,
or without a single soldier, exhibits a more
forbidding posture to foreign ambition
than America disunited, with a hundred
thousand veterans ready for combat."

JAMES MADISON, *THE FEDERALIST PAPERS*, NOVEMBER 30, 1787

"Upon [America's] preservation must depend our own
happiness and that of countless generations to come.
Whatever dangers may threaten it, I shall stand by it and
maintain it in its integrity to the full extent of the obligations
mposed and the power conferred upon me by the Constitution."

ZACHARY TAYLOR

"To those who cling to power through corruption
and deceit and the silencing of dissent,
know that you are on the wrong side of history;
but that we will extend a hand if you are
willing to unclench your fist."

BARACK OBAMA

"Observe good faith and justice
towards all Nations. Cultivate peace
and harmony with all."

GEORGE WASHINGTON, FAREWELL ADDRESS, SEPTEMBER 19, 1796

"Peace is not made at the Council table or by treaties,
but in the hearts of men."

HERBERT HOOVER

"Whether we bring our enemies to justice,
or bring justice to our enemies,
justice will be done."

GEORGE W. BUSH

Even as a battle-hardened Civil War general, **Ulysses S. Gra**
couldn't stand the sight of blood. Men who served with him note
turned away from gory battlefields and even had his meat cooke
oint of charring—if there was even a trace of blood, he'd lose his

Woodrow Wilson kept a herd of sheep to mow the White House lawn during World War I. The animals were a powerful and practical symbol of home-front support for troops abroad. Not only did they save on manpower needed to keep the grass trimmed, they also provided a source of wool for Red Cross bandages. Wilson was often spotted patting the sheep's heads as he passed.

★ ★ ★ ★ ★ ★ ★

"The world must be made safe for democracy. Its peace must be planted upon the tested foundations of political liberty. We have no selfish ends to serve. We desire no conquest, no dominion. We seek no indemnities for ourselves, no material compensation for the sacrifices we shall freely make."

WOODROW WILSON
IN HIS ADDRESS TO CONGRESS ASKING FOR A DECLARATION OF WAR, 1917

"I have never advocated war except as a means of peace."

ULYSSES S. GRANT

"Dante reserved a special place of infamy in the inferno for those base angels who dared side neither with evil nor with good. Peace is ardently to be desired, but only as the handmaid of righteousness."

THEODORE ROOSEVELT

Three presidents attended military academies:

Ulysses S. Grant
(U.S. Military Academy at West Point, 1843)
Dwight D. Eisenhower
(West Point, 1915)
Jimmy Carter
(U.S. Naval Academy at Annapolis, 1946)

★ ★ ★ ★ ★ ★ ★ ★ ★

LITTLE DID YOU KNOW...

The presidency was only one of **Gerald R. Ford**'s diverse jobs. While earning a law degree at Yale, he coached the football and boxing teams. He was also a ranger in Yellowstone National Park, where his favorite duties were checking park vehicles every morning and taking up arms as a guard on the bear-feeding trucks. Service on an aircraft carrier during World War II and success as a lawyer add to his varied résumé. He turned down offers from two professional football teams, though.

George H. W. Bush joined the armed forces
as soon as he graduated from high school.
At nineteen, he was the youngest Navy pilot.
He fought in World War II, flying fifty-eight combat missions.
He painted the name of his wife, Barbara, on the side of his plane.

Dwight D. Eisenhower was the only president
to serve in both world wars.

"It would be judicious to act with magnanimity towards a prostrate foe."

ZACHARY TAYLOR

"In the time of darkest defeat,
victory may be nearest."

WILLIAM MCKINLEY

"An honorable defeat is better
than a dishonorable victory."

MILLARD FILLMORE

"May our country be always successful,
but whether successful or otherwise, always right."

JOHN QUINCY ADAMS

"We have become great because of the lavish use of our resources. But the time has come to inquire seriously what will happen when our forests are gone, when the coal, the iron, the oil, and the gas are exhausted, when the soils shall have been still further impoverished and washed into the streams, polluting the rivers, denuding the fields, and obstructing navigation."

THEODORE ROOSEVELT

"We must not only protect the countryside and save it from destruction, we must restore what has been destroyed.... Once our natural splendor is destroyed, it can never be recaptured. And once man can no longer walk with beauty or wonder at nature, his spirit will wither and his sustenance be wasted."

LYNDON B. JOHNSON

"We have fallen heirs to the most glorious heritage a people ever received, and each one must do his part if we wish to show that the nation is worthy of its good fortune."

THEODORE ROOSEVELT

"Laws change; people die;
the land remains."

ABRAHAM LINCOLN

"It is the course of wisdom to set aside an ample portion of our natural resources as national parks and reserves, thus ensuring that future generations may know the majesty of the Earth as we know it today."

JOHN F. KENNEDY

Vice President Chester A. Arthur takes the oath of office after the death of President James A. Garfield, as depicted in *Frank Leslie's Illustrated Newspaper*, 1881.

PERSONAL LIVES & DEATHS

★ ★

The men, the myths, and the presidential records

Harry S. Truman's middle initial doesn't stand for a name. His parents put the "S" there to honor his grandfathers, Solomon Young and Anderson Shipp Truman.

This has caused controversy since Truman's lifetime. Should there be a period after the initial, even though it's not short for anything? Archivists at the Harry S. Truman Presidential Library and Museum say they still get this question. The library's website has a page explaining why there should indeed be a period.

If you're elected president, chances are you'll pick up a nickname or two along the way. Arguably, some of the best include William H. Harrison as "Old Tippecanoe," Martin Van Buren as "The Little Magician" and the "Red Fox of Kinderhook," and Grover Cleveland as "Big Steve" and "Uncle Jumbo."

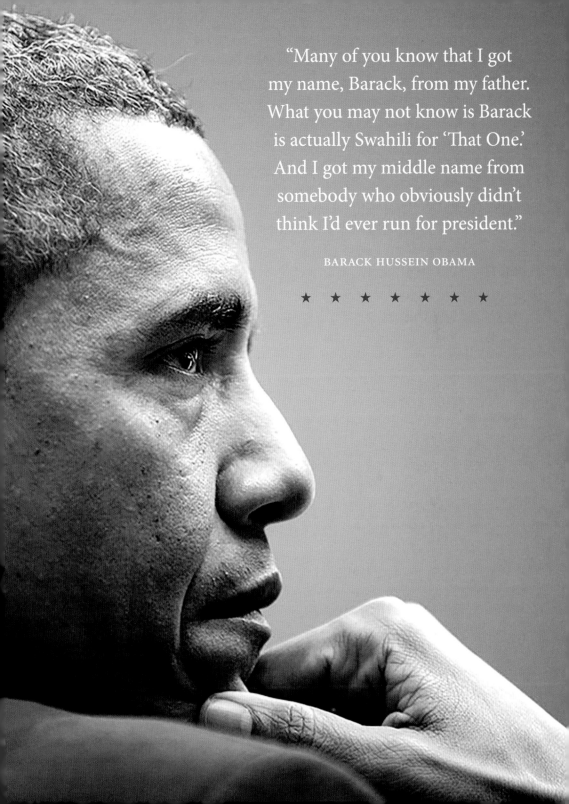

"Many of you know that I got my name, Barack, from my father. What you may not know is Barack is actually Swahili for 'That One.' And I got my middle name from somebody who obviously didn't think I'd ever run for president."

BARACK HUSSEIN OBAMA

★ ★ ★ ★ ★ ★ ★

Lyndon B. Johnson's entire family
shared the initials "LBJ":
his wife, Lady Bird, their daughters,
Lynda Bird and Luci Baines,
and even Little Beagle the dog.

★ ★ ★

NEW YORK
NEW YORK
MUTUAL
ABC NEWS
HOORAY
CONNECTICUT
TENNESSEE FOR LBJ
LBJ FOR THE USA
We Are 4 YOU
LBJ

"I may be president of the United States, but my private life is nobody's damned business."

CHESTER A. ARTHUR

"If my superiors shall permit me to come home, I hope it will be soon; if they mean I should stay abroad, I am not able to say what I shall do, until I know in what capacity. One thing is certain, that I will not live long without my family."

JOHN ADAMS, LETTER TO ABIGAIL ADAMS, AUGUST 13, 1783

"Mothers all want their sons to grow up to be president, but they don't want them to become politicians in the process."

JOHN F. KENNEDY

"The great Searcher of human hearts
is my witness, that I have no wish,
which aspires beyond the humble and happy
lot of living and dying a private citizen
on my own farm."

GEORGE WASHINGTON, LETTER TO CHARLES PETTIT, AUGUST 16, 1788

Grover Cleveland is the only president to get married in the White House. He was uncomfortable living there as a bachelor, so he took his ward, age twenty-one, as his wife.
She became the youngest First Lady.
In spite of many raised eyebrows from all sides,
the couple appears to have led a happy married life,
raising five children in the presidential mansion.

One of the best-beloved pets at Theodore Roosevelt's
White House was Algonquin the piebald pony.
Once, when young Archie Roosevelt was sick,
his brothers Kermit and Quentin thought they'd
cheer him up. Since they couldn't bring their brother
to see his pony, they brought the pony up to the boy…
in the White House elevator.

Abraham Lincoln received over ten thousand death threats during his presidency. A few he kept in his desk in an envelope labeled "Assassinations."

William McKinley was known for his distinctive "McKinley grip," a method of speedily shaking hands with well-wishers in a receiving line. He would take the right hand as usual, and place his left on the greeter's elbow to send him on his way. This was, as it happened, his final action. At a reception for the Pan-American Exposition in Buffalo, New York, in September 1901, McKinley's assassin approached him, a hankerchief covering his extended hand. When the president reached out to shake it, the assassin whipped off the covering to expose a gun and shot McKinley.

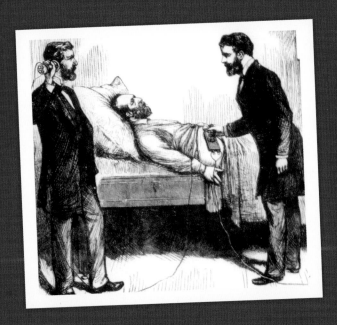

After an assassin shot **James A. Garfield,** he lived for more than two months before dying from complications. Alexander Graham Bell created a metal detector specifically to find the bullet that no amount of probing doctors could. Unfortunately, steel coils in the mattress on which the dying president lay made the instrument malfunction and fail to locate the bullet.

William H. Taft takes first prize for largest president at 325 pounds. In fact, he often got stuck in the White House bathtub, and so had a custom-sized replacement installed to save White House staff from having to get him out.

★ ★ ★ ★ ★ ★ ★

John F. Kennedy holds many presidential records. He was the first president to be born in the twentieth century, the only Roman Catholic president, and the only one to win a Pulitzer Prize. He was, at 43, the youngest elected president, and when he died less than three years later, he was, unfortunately, the youngest president to die.

Joe Biden was 78 years old when he was sworn in as the 46th president in January 2021, making him the oldest serving president.

George W. Bush graduated from Harvard Business School, making him the only president to hold a master's degree in business administration.

James Buchanan never married and was the first bachelor to serve as president.

"I'm a great believer in luck, and I find the harder I work, the more I have of it."

THOMAS JEFFERSON IS COMMONLY CREDITED WITH THIS PHRASE, THOUGH ITS EARLIEST APPEARANCE WAS 1922.

"Elevate them guns a little lower."

ANDREW JACKSON,
OFTEN MOCKED FOR HIS SUPPOSED INTELLECTUAL LIMITATIONS,
HAS BEEN SADDLED OVER THE YEARS WITH MANY INANITIES SUCH AS THIS ONE.

"When you get to the end of your rope, tie a knot and hang on."

ABRAHAM LINCOLN AND BOTH THE ROOSEVELT PRESIDENTS ARE BELIEVED TO HAVE SAID THIS.

"It is amazing what you can accomplish if you do not care who gets the credit."

FITTINGLY, NO ONE SEEMS TO CARE WHO GETS CREDIT FOR THIS POPULAR IDEA—
THE LIST INCLUDES HARRY S. TRUMAN AND RONALD REAGAN,
BUT ITS PROVENANCE IS LIKELY VARIABLE.

President-elect Harry S. Truman holds up an edition of the *Chicago Daily Tribune* proclaiming "Dewey Defeats Truman." Oops.

★THE PRESIDENTS★

1. George Washington (1732–1799). Served in office: 1789–1797. Independent/no party affiliation, Virginia. Noted for his exemplary service as the first president, his role as the commander in chief who led the American colonies to victory and nationhood, and for his status as perhaps the most universally admired American president.

2. John Adams (1735–1826). Served in office: 1797–1801. Federalist, Massachusetts. Noted for his success as a lawyer, his strengths as a political philosopher, and the role he took as a Founding Father, particularly in promoting the Declaration of Independence in Congress. He is considered "Father of the American Navy."

3. Thomas Jefferson (1743–1826). Served in office: 1801–1809. Democratic-Republican, Virginia. Noted for his role as a Founding Father and author of the Declaration of Independence, making the Louisiana Purchase and sending Lewis and Clark to document it, and significantly reducing the national debt.

4. **James Madison** (1751–1836). Served in office: 1809–1817. Democratic-Republican, Virginia. Noted for his role as a Founding Father and "Father of the Constitution," his coauthorship of the Bill of Rights and The Federalist Papers, and his keen handling of the War of 1812.

5. **James Monroe** (1758–1831). Served in office: 1817–1825. Democratic-Republican, Virginia. Noted for being the last Founding Father president, the Monroe Doctrine against foreign interference in the Americas, expanding U.S. territory, and presiding over the "Era of Good Feelings."

6. **John Quincy Adams** (1767–1848). Served in office: 1825–1829. Democratic-Republican, Massachusetts. Noted for developing and implementing the fundamentals of U.S. foreign policy, including negotiating the Treaty of Ghent to end the War of 1812 with Britain; overseeing the Chesapeake & Ohio Canal; and modernizing the economy.

7. Andrew Jackson (1767–1845). Served in office: 1829–1837. Democrat, Tennessee. Noted for battling the banks, culminating in his veto against the U.S. Bank's charter; for supporting and signing the Indian Removal Act; and for ending the Nullification Crisis by refusing to let South Carolina secede.

8. Martin Van Buren (1782–1862). Served in office: 1837–1841. Democrat, New York. Noted for championing the two-party system, solidifying the Democratic party, and attempting to institute an independent treasury in response to the financial "Panic of 1837."

9. William H. Harrison (1773–1841). Served in office: March 1841–April 1841. Whig, Ohio. Noted for initiating now-standard campaign strategies and for dying from the cold he caught at his inauguration, establishing the precedent for presidential funerals and succession.

10. John Tyler (1790–1862). Served in office: 1841–1845. Whig and then Independent, Virginia. Noted for initiating the annexation of Texas, for encouraging westward settlement, and for being the first to ascend to the presidency without election.

11. James K. Polk (1795–1849). Served in office: 1845–1849. Democrat, Tennessee. Noted for greatly expanding U.S. territory under the doctrine of "Manifest Destiny"; for increasing tensions with other nations, culminating in the Mexican-American War; and for achieving everything on his presidential to-do list.

12. Zachary Taylor (1784–1850). Served in office: 1849–1850. Whig, Louisiana. Noted for his unflappable nature, for his military prowess before the presidency, and for facing down increased North-South tensions by forbidding secession.

13. Millard Fillmore (1800–1874). Served in office: 1850–1853. Whig, New York. Noted for being the last president not to be a Democrat or Republican, and for supporting the Compromise of 1850, which included the Fugitive Slave Act and delayed a culmination of the slavery "Crisis of 1850."

14. Franklin Pierce (1804–1869). Served in office: 1853–1857. Democrat, New Hampshire. Noted for replacing the Missouri Compromise with the Kansas-Nebraska Act, leading to increased conflicts over slavery.

15. James Buchanan (1791–1868). Served in office: 1857–1861. Democrat, Pennsylvania. Noted for attempting to maintain peace between the states, but ultimately failing to solve divisive issues and leaving the country on the tipping point of crisis.

16. Abraham Lincoln (1809–1865). Served in office: 1861–1865. Republican, Illinois. Noted for bringing an end to slavery; for leading the nation, intact, through perhaps its most tumultuous times; and for general presidential prowess.

17. Andrew Johnson (1808–1875). Served in office: 1865–1869. Democrat, Tennessee. Noted for favoring a quick restoration of seceded states to the Union after the Civil War.

18. Ulysses S. Grant (1822–1885). Served in office: 1869–1877. Republican, Illinois. Noted for leading the Union Army to victory as a general, and, as president, for leading efforts to remove the remnants of slavery and Confederate nationalism, to protect African American citizenship, and to promote economic prosperity.

19. Rutherford B. Hayes (1822–1893). Served in office: 1877–1881. Republican, Ohio. Noted for overseeing the reunification of the country during the tail end of Reconstruction.

20. James A. Garfield (1831–1881). Served in office: March 1881– September 1881. Republican, Ohio. Noted for an assassination attempt, followed by over two months of prolonged suffering before he finally died from complications.

21. Chester A. Arthur (1829–1886). Served in office: 1881–1885. Republican, New York. Noted for his efforts in civil service reform.

22 & 24. Grover Cleveland (1837–1908). Served in office: 1885–1889 and 1893–1897. Democrat, New York. Noted for his nonconsecutive terms and his emphasis on political reform and fiscal conservatism.

23. Benjamin Harrison (1833–1901). Served in office: 1889–1893. Republican, Indiana. Noted for economic legislation, including the Sherman Antitrust Act, for aiding in the creation of National Forests, and for an active foreign policy.

25. William McKinley (1843–1901). Served in office: 1897–1901. Republican, Ohio. Noted for leading a U.S. victory in the Spanish-American War, for raising protective tariffs to promote American industry, and for rejecting inflation by keeping the gold standard.

26. Theodore Roosevelt (1858–1919). Served in office: 1901–1909. Republican, New York. Noted for his contributions to environment conservation, including the protection of about 230 million acres of public land; for his foreign policy efforts; and for his "Square Deal" legislation.

27. William H. Taft (1857–1930). Served in office: 1909–1913. Republican, Ohio. Noted for expanding Roosevelt's antitrust policies and the Civil Service, for creating the Department of Labor, and for pursuing "Dollar Diplomacy" abroad.

28. Woodrow Wilson (1856–1924). Served in office: 1913–1921. Democrat, New Jersey. Noted for his "New Freedom" progressive legislature, his leadership and striving for peace during World War I, his negotiation of the Treaty of Versailles, and his founding role in the League of Nations.

29. Warren G. Harding (1865–1923). Served in office: 1921–1923. Republican, Ohio. Noted for promising a "return to normalcy," sponsoring the first disarmament conference in the Washington Naval Conference, and suffering dishonor due to corrupt advisers.

30. Calvin Coolidge (1872–1933). Served in office: 1923–1929. Republican, Vermont and Massachusetts. Noted for restoring public faith in the presidency, for his laissez-faire style, and for supporting the international Kellogg-Briand Pact.

31. Herbert Hoover (1874–1964). Served in office: 1929–1933. Republican, California. Noted for being ineffective in the face of economic disaster, hand in hand with a small-government approach and championing of "rugged individualism" that did not improve Great Depression conditions.

32. Franklin D. Roosevelt (1882–1945). Served in office: 1933–1945. Democrat, New York. Noted for the "New Deal" government aid programs aimed at combatting the Depression, his leadership during World War II, and his peace efforts for its aftermath, including an instrumental role in developing the United Nations.

33. Harry S. Truman (1884–1972). Served in office: 1945–1953. Democrat, Missouri. Noted for leading the nation through the end of World War II, supporting an internationalist foreign policy, establishing the "Truman Doctrine" against the spread of communism, overseeing the creation of several new defense and security departments, and for his "Fair Deal" domestic policy.

34. Dwight D. Eisenhower (1890–1969). Served in office: 1953–1961. Republican, New York and Kansas. Noted for attempting to improve Soviet relations, but actually launching the arms race; signing Civil Rights Acts and overseeing desegregation; and expanding New Deal and Fair Deal initiatives.

35. John F. Kennedy (1917–1963). Served in office: 1961–1963. Democrat, Massachusetts. Noted for his "New Frontier" policies, most significantly focused on civil rights, international aid, and space exploration, and his leadership through the Cuban Missile Crisis, Bay of Pigs Invasion, and signing of the Test Ban Treaty.

36. Lyndon B. Johnson (1908–1973). Served in office: 1963–1969. Democrat, Texas. Noted for his "Great Society" policies, including the "war on poverty," and for significantly increasing American involvement in the Vietnam War.

37. Richard M. Nixon (1913–1994).
Served in office: 1969–1974. Republican,
California. Noted for escalating and then
ending U.S. involvement in Vietnam, for
initiating détente with Russia and diplomatic
relations with China, and for resigning in
disgrace after the Watergate scandal.

38. Gerald R. Ford (1913–2006). Served in office: 1974–1977.
Republican, Michigan. Noted for his controversial pardon of Nixon,
for continuing détente through the Helsinki Accords, and for
increasing congressional involvement in foreign affairs.

39. Jimmy Carter (b. 1924).
Served in office: 1977–1981. Democrat,
Georgia. Noted for mediating the Camp
David Accords, creating the Department
of Energy, and overseeing increased
environmental protection.

40. **Ronald Reagan** (1911–2004). Served in office: 1981–1989. Republican, California. Noted for restoring the economy, championing the "trickle down" effect, emphasizing national defense and military initiatives, leading the thaw of the Cold War, and dealing with the Iran-Contra affair.

41. **George H. W. Bush** (1924–2018). Served in office: 1989–1993. Republican, Texas. Noted for a heavy emphasis on foreign policy, including the maintenance of peace with the Soviet Union even as it collapsed; leadership during the Persian Gulf War; and involvement in Panama.

42. **Bill Clinton** (b. 1946). Served in office: 1993–2001. Democrat, Arkansas. Noted for signing the North American Free Trade Agreement, for health care reform, for conservative economic policies, and for foreign interventions in Haiti, Iraq, and Serbia.

43. **George W. Bush** (b. 1946). Served in office: 2001–2009. Republican, Texas. Noted for declaring a "War on Terror" following the 9/11 attacks, with U.S. involvement in Afghanistan and Iraq; for signing the Patriot Act and educational reform legislation; and for facing the "Great Recession."

44. **Barack Obama** (b. 1961). Served in office: 2009–2017. Democrat, Illinois. Noted for health care reforms, efforts to aid the economy, overseeing continued military involvement abroad, and supporting progressive social policies.

45. **Donald J. Trump** (b. 1946). Served in office: 2017–2021. Republican, New York. Noted for his unconventional style, being in office at the start of the Covid-19 global pandemic, and being impeached, and acquitted, twice.

46. **Joe Biden** (b. 1942). Served in office: 2021–. Democrat, Delaware. Noted for his bipartisan approach to governing, thanks to a thirty-six-year tenure in the Senate and eight years as vice president.

About Appleseed Press Book Publishers

Great ideas grow over time. From seed to harvest,
Appleseed Press brings fine reading and entertainment
together between the covers of its creatively crafted books.
Our grove bears fruit twice a year, publishing a new
crop of titles each Spring and Fall.

Visit us online at
appleseedpressbooks.com
or write to us at
68 North Street
Kennebunkport, Maine 04046